YELLOW ARROW

Vol. X, No. 2
Fall 2025
Kairos

Yellow Arrow Journal

Creative nonfiction, poetry, and cover art by writers and
artists identifying as women

Vol. X, No. 2
Fall 2025
Kairos

Editor-in-Chief
Kapua Iao

Creative Director
Alexa Laharty

Guest Editor
Darah Schillinger

KAIROS Editorial Team

Hannah Bishoff, Jill Earl, Jennifer M. Eyre, Meg Gamble,
Siobhan McKenna, Leticia Priebe Rocha, Kait Quinn,
Nicky Ruddell, Mel Silberger, Beck Snyder, and Avery Wood

Contributors

Stephanie Anderson, Aileen Bassis, Deepti Bhatia, Loretta Cantieri,
Roxanne Christiana, Virginia Ottley Craighill,
Patricia Davis-Muffett, Amy Devine, Johanna Elattar,
Renee Emerson, Pratibha Kumari Gupta, Taylor Harrison,
Elizabeth Hazen, Jennifer Randall Hotz, Cam McGlynn, Gloria Ogo,
Rebecca Hart Olander, Giulia Paglione, Danielle Salerno,
Hillary Smith-Maddern, erica r. such, Vivian Walman-Randall,
Kathleen Weed, Katharine Weinmann, Audrey J. Whitson,
Keri Withington, Chelsea Yates, and Kristin Camitta Zimet

Cover Artist
Clara Garza

YELLOW ARROW

PUBLISHING

PO Box 65185, Baltimore, MD 21209
info@yellowarrowpublishing.com

Yellow Arrow Journal - Kairos

ISBN (paperback): 979-8-9883176-9-2
ISSN (print): 2688-3015
ISSN (online): 2688-3023

Cover art by Clara Garza.
Cover and interior design by Yellow Arrow Publishing.
For more information, see yellowarrowpublishing.com.

*We prioritize the unique voice and
style of each of our authors.*

*Every writer has a story to tell and
every story is worth telling.*

Yellow Arrow Publishing

Two Familiar Strangers
Gloria Ogo

It wasn't a car crash
or a phone call in the night.
Just a quiet Tuesday
when she forgot
my name.

She looked at me
like I was someone
who had knocked on her door
asking for directions—
polite, curious,
but far away.

That was the moment.
The shift.
When I realized
everything we build—
stories, memory, even love—
can thin like paper
if held too long in the sun.

I didn't cry right away.
I made her tea.
I laughed at a joke
she didn't finish.
I told myself:
this is just a bad day.

But it kept happening.
Names slipped.
Seasons confused her.
She called me her sister,
then a neighbor,
then no one.

Now, I try to remember.
Not just her
but who I was
before I learned
that time can fold in on itself.

Looking for the parts
of her that remain
in how I stir the tea,
in the lullaby,
in the way I still say her name
even when she doesn't say mine.

Table of Contents

Dear Readers,

A few days ago, one of my coworkers gave me a miniature orchid for my birthday. The instructions on the tag state to give the orchid one ice cube a week, the equivalent of 1.5 tablespoons of water. As I write this, the flower sits, outstretched toward me like a hand begging for food. Out of laziness, or forgetfulness, or my inherent inability to keep houseplants alive, I have yet to offer it an ice cube. With each day that passes, the leaves yellow like a bruise.

Most of my writing pulls inspiration from my own life and since starting a full-time job I've found my motivation to cultivate creativity has all but gone. My fiction feels forced, my poetry uninspired. I stare at blank pages the same way I stare at the dry soil of my desk plant, knowing I should search for water but still leaving it to wilt and die. So when I was asked to be the guest editor for *Yellow Arrow Journal* Vol. X, No. 2, I realized this was the perfect opportunity to push myself, and others, to till the soil and grow something new.

When I edit for a magazine or journal, one of the hardest responsibilities is narrowing down what pieces to include in an issue. I knew going into the process that there would be some thoughtful, painful, funny, beautiful, grief-stricken, and/or contemplative works that would inevitably be rejected for one reason or another. And as I read through the submissions we received in August for **KAIROS**, the theme chosen by the team, I was delighted and burdened by the realization that our writing community is full of inspired contributors with worthy stories to tell. And while I may have struggled to let certain pieces go, I am confident that the pieces in this issue hold a depth, honesty, and imagination that feel right for *this* issue.

The concept of **KAIROS**—the timeliness of a moment or memory—is central to this collection because it is central to the act of creation. These are works that emerged now because *now* was the time to write them, and as I reread each piece within the issue, I am struck by how deeply personal and yet widely resonant they are. In these pages, you'll find contributors who are navigating memory, grief, identity, and change—not to relive the past but to better understand how it informs who they are and who they could become.

Being the guest editor for *Yellow Arrow Journal* has been a unique privilege, having started as an editorial intern with Yellow Arrow before transitioning to a chapbook author, then guest speaker, and returning to where I feel most comfortable: uplifting the works of others. Before you delve into this issue, I want to take a moment to say thank you for reading, for supporting this incredible community of women-presenting creatives, and for inspiring me to cultivate my writing (and my new orchid). I hope you find something in this volume that inspires your own moment of reflection and encourages you to jot it down. You never know what a moment can grow into.

With Gratitude,

Darah Schillinger

KAIROS

~ KAIROS ~

a time when conditions are right
for the accomplishment of a crucial
action; an opportune and decisive
moment; in modern Greek, also
"weather" or "time"; in ancient Greek,
"the right or critical moment"

Fatherland
Taylor Harrison

The kosher salt sand slipped through my fingers as I watched the tide receding, the cerulean sea on the westernmost edge of North America clear and enticing but treacherous. Our hotel concierge told us that if we wanted to swim, it would be at our own risk. I palmed another fistful of coarse earth, remnants of the past crushed up and transmogrified into seaside treasures: shattered stones, empty shells, and flakes of coral, once singular and whole. I felt the galaxy of pebbles beneath my feet, the cyclical crashing of the tide shaping the oceanic universe.

I wondered if my ancestors had walked these beaches, or if they had ever even made it to the Baja California peninsula, hailing from the Mexican states of Tlaxcala and Jalisco, crossing the border into San Ysidro and settling in San Diego, California, in the latter half of the 20th century. I considered how it was my first time in Los Cabos, Mexico, despite my familial history in this country, insulated by an all-inclusive, European-owned resort, saying niceties in Spanish gleaned from my required high school Spanish courses, but switching to English because I was ashamed that I was mostly monolingual. "Hola," I'd start when meeting new people. "¿Cómo estás?" I quickly realized that I had forgotten that I should be referring to strangers in the formal "usted" form of "you" instead of "tú," and then I stopped greeting locals altogether.

****

Growing up, I did not know about my Mexican ancestry. My last name was of French origin, despite my father receiving mail bearing a surname commonly found in Mexico. It was said that it was likely due to a repeat clerical error or a case of mistaken identity. My grandfather, who had a thick, ambiguous accent, was once asked by a family friend's parent if he was Mexican. Offended, he shouted, "How could you even think that? We're

French!" After that, everyone around us knew better than to question our cultural background.

My father spoke fluent Spanish and, as a child, spent summers in Mexico. He claimed on more than one occasion that he also spoke French and German, though I never heard a single utterance from him in either tongue. A few months before I found out about my hidden heritage, my father casually revealed that my great-grandmother was French and happened to give birth to my grandfather while vacationing in Mexico, and then settled there, which was why we had family in that region to begin with. As a 10-year-old, I had no reason to be suspicious. He refused to speak about my grandmother, who passed away from cancer before I was born, but the assumption was that she was also of European origin.

Throughout my childhood, I was often asked where I was "from." When I grew older, the word "exotic" would appear as a veiled compliment in some suitors' vernacular to both my sister and me. *Like a car*, I used to think. *An object to behold.* I had waist-length black hair, a large nose, dark eyes, and pallid skin, several features that infringed upon Eurocentric beauty standards. In addition to my mother's half-Syrian side, I would list out about a dozen European countries to inquiring adults, with one teacher encouraging me to write down my cultural heritage in case I forgot.

"You know," my dad used to say when asked about our family, "we're just a little bit of everything—mostly European." I didn't question him, but in hindsight, he found other ways to covertly share the truth with me. One time, when we were on the subject of doppelgängers, my father said I might have one in Mexico, and I thought that was unexpected given our purported roots in France. On the weekends when we would run errands, he'd play mariachi music, the melodies interspersed with his playlist of alternative '80s tracks. I fell in love with the emotion behind each song despite my inability to understand the words, basking in the resonance that would hang in the air long after the music had ended. Perhaps it was him showing, not telling, to try and foster an organic connection to our secret history and long-silenced ancestors.

My grandfather died a couple of months after I turned 11, coinciding with when my father came clean about our origins. Our French identities had been fabricated. It turned out that Dad was about 10 years old when his last name was legally changed to a French surname to avoid discrimination and help with assimilation. My grandfather was never a police chief, or pilot, or World War II veteran—or any of the other heroic jobs he had shared with our family—but a humble car painter, as indicated by the naturalization paperwork I later found online. My grandmother was not Henriette, but Enriqueta. She was from Guadalajara, my grandfather from Apizaco. My father's siblings had been born in Mexico, though he had been born the year they immigrated to the United States. Finally, I learned that my father spent the first years of his life in a multicultural neighborhood in south San Diego, where the state sliced through the quaint street of bungalows to pave the way for the Interstate 5 freeway when my father was a toddler, a devastating act that widely displaced communities of color in the mid-20th century. They later moved to Orange County, where I was raised.

When I began to embrace my heritage in my teens and young adulthood, I often felt I wasn't Mexican *enough*. I was brought into a diversity-and-inclusion exercise at work, where my colleagues spoke of their upbringings and planned how we would celebrate Hispanic Heritage Month through recipes, Hispanic and Latino cultural observances, and stories about our countries of origin. I had nothing to offer other than words of encouragement and my yearning to learn more, leading me to feel as fraudulent as my father must have when he entered the fifth grade with a fancy new French last name, one that might as well have been picked out of a hat. Was I *faking* this tie to my ancestral lands?

****

After baking on the beach for two days, my husband and I finally left the resort to visit the downtown area of San José del Cabo, enticed by the opportunity to visit art galleries and experience more of Mexico. The city center was a rainbow of papel picado flags, each street more bewitching than the last. We met a local jeweler who crafted fine jewelry in bronze, gold, and silver, infusing each avant-garde piece with an array of animal-derived elements and precious stones. We meandered through the cobbled streets and exchanged music recommendations with the owner of a record store, who had one of the most curated collections I had ever laid eyes on. Then we entered a hybrid café and gift store and began a long conversation with the owner, her face framed by long highlighted tendrils. She had opened the shop more than two decades ago.

"Where are you from?" she asked my husband, who grew up in a small northern town on the border of England and Wales. She then looked at me and stopped. "So, you're American," she stared intently at me. "And what else?"

I began an uninhibited monologue of my backstory, apologizing for not speaking Spanish and for the ambiguity that colored my familial past; for being a poor excuse of a person with ties to this beautiful land, this land I didn't fully deserve because I had never known it in the way my family had; for being someone who took the privilege of my European last name for granted, who would have been better off having been bestowed the generational artifact of my cultural history; who knew no traditions and had no contact with the dozens of cousins and extended family members who did not know of my existence.

She smiled warmly, adjusting her hair to the other shoulder. After a long pause, she said, "It's okay—you shouldn't worry about that." She continued, "My nieces who live in the States don't speak Spanish either. You can always learn."

She asked which parts of Mexico my father's side was from and shared that she was visiting Guadalajara that summer. "You must go," she said. "It's an incredible place."

I self-consciously beamed, realizing that she was right. It wasn't too late, and it never would be, though I was cautious as I considered her words. First, I had to do the work. But this thought of not being "enough" of anything was fruitless and rooted in colonialist ideals: this is who I am and always have been. The blood of my ancestors runs through my veins. Their sweat pours in rivulets down my spine. Their tears are my own. It can be true that I am both American and descended from generations of people from disparate lands. I am not permanently locked out of my culture, because I *am* my culture. And there was much, much more to discover beyond a short vacation to Los Cabos.

My husband and I purchased an art print of Plaza Mijares as a souvenir and then patronized other shops and restaurants, concluding our day with two mezcalitas. In another shop window, I locked eyes with a young woman who looked like she could be a family member of mine. Intoxicated by the alcohol and the town, I photographed every building, not wanting to forget where I had been and where I pledged to return in the years to come.

We retired to the beach that night and this time, I felt lighter in basking in my true reverence for the gilded gravel beneath my feet, the country that allowed for generations of people before me to survive. I thought of the jeweler we had met that afternoon and his seashells and bones and 24-karat gold. I hoped to one day be turned into one of his pieces, to become one with my ancestral lands and part of an amalgamated treasure.

COLONIZING MARS

Roxanne Christiana

Your car fishtailed in the slush
that was already
beginning to freeze,
as if you couldn't wait
to get away after
dropping me off at
the library
on Christmas Eve.

I had just started reading
the books I checked out
when the librarian
flashed the lights before closing,
and I found myself
back on the street again,
at twilight,
waiting for you.

The snow was falling faster,
soft as the pages
tucked under my arm,
but the cold got into my shoes.
I shifted the books
from hand to hand,
too proud to set them down,
too cold to feel my fingers,
and still no sign of your car.

The church bells had tolled nine
by the time you showed up—
not in your car,
but in a taxi
because you'd forgotten
where you parked.
You smelled like whiskey and snow,
and swung the door wide
and invited me in.

Mom was almost finished
decorating the tree
when you stumbled and fell
into it and brought it down,
glass breaking like a gasp.
She dragged you around
the living room by your ear,
while the tree leaned drunkenly
against the sofa,
twinkling sideways,
its broken ornaments catching
what little light was left.

I took my books to my room
without a word,
curled up beneath the covers
and opened the one
on colonizing Mars.
Outside, snow kept falling
like nothing had happened.
I could hear you arguing
through the wall, and the tree
never stood quite right
for the rest of that year.

Last Poem for My Father
Virginia Ottley Craighill

I thought I was through with you. Spent years
of your steady decline pouring out grief
and anger. Death was a welcome silence.
But this night in a nameless posada
outside a nameless town on the Camino,
I dream of you, my father: you're dreaming,
limbs moving in some somatic chase
like an old dog still hunting in its sleep.
I wake you. You turn to my friend Karen,
say her name. She reads a poem; I lift you,
light as a child, hold your frail weight in my lap.
We watch a rainbow while words comfort us.
I awake crying to the sound of cattle
bells clanging outside my window, darkness.
Why did it take so long, this forgiveness?
No matter. Tomorrow, I move on.

The Second Abortion

Loretta Cantieri

The tissue
enmeshed
with my womb
belies
you are
separate
from me

as a thin
rod-like
instrument
dilates my cervix

my mind shuts down,
a loud
steel gate,
square, white
pockmarked
ceiling tiles

I close my eyes,
morning light
on a field
of milkweed,
the crevice
of each pod
covered with
orange beetles

painfully
opened
now,
my uterus is
no longer protected

the sun on
purple lilacs
by the junior
high, I
stuff the basket
of my bike
with flowers
for my mother

"breathe deep
count to ten,
you are not
breathing"

my legs
secure
in stirrups,
my thighs
tremble like
a worker's arm
on a jackhammer

I ask, "can't we wait,
one more minute"

"no, your cervix is dilated"

I hear the machine
for the second time,
my uterus a sheet
flapping in a gusty wind.

Past Life

Elizabeth Hazen

As orange darkened to purple, bats emerged, first a couple,
and then a great colony that click-click-clicked past me, flitting
under the overhang, so close I captured one's face with a snap of
my Kodak camera. It was August 2003, and I was at an artist's
retreat in northern Pennsylvania, staying in a white clapboard
church that had been converted into studios. At a desk that
had been a pew, I worked on poems about my friend Flynn, a
mild-mannered poet who loved Frank O'Hara and the band The
Magnetic Fields, and who, mired too long in despair, had killed
himself that March. Somehow, I found my way to the retreat a
few months later. There was no internet at the church back then,
and I had no cell phone. The television that was there showed
only static, so at dusk I sat outside and watched the bats.

They would dart around like pinballs, completely indifferent
to me. Grief was a constant, but the bats elicited no fear. I felt
kinship with these creatures who were unlike other mammals. I
had never seen any in Baltimore, though in 2003 little brown bats
were common in western Pennsylvania, vast numbers cruising
for insects through the evening skies. For years after the retreat, I
clung to the memory of those nights under the soaring bats.

In 2023 I returned to the retreat at the church, excited to
relive those evenings. After 20 years Flynn's death was more scar
than bruise, and it was the absence of pain that grieved me, as if
I had lost him all over again. But the magic of the bats was still
fresh in my mind, and I wanted to reclaim that wonder.

Of course, things for me have changed over the decades. I
have a teenage son now. I am divorced and remarried. I've tried
several different jobs. For six years, I drank far too much and
then stopped drinking. I've lost loved ones to arguments
and distance and death. Others have stayed close, and we moved
through the years in parallel, largely oblivious to how much

is changing, like sleeping passengers on an airplane who have forgotten they are moving at all.

The church itself had only changed a little. The kitchen had been updated, and the downstairs area where I had written was now divided into a living room and bedroom. The pew-desk was gone. The porch was now contained by a shoddy fence, and beyond that, a bush had grown so big it obscured my view of the farmhouse down the hill. Mostly, though, the place was the same.

Every night at the retreat, I waited, an occasional swallow giving false hope, but the bats never came. Dusk after dusk, I made do with the bumbling groundhog and peppy rabbits that crisscrossed the grass. But no bats. In the daylight hours, I found new sources of magic: the hilly Pennsylvania roads, the way the wind in the grass created a shimmering, flashes of whitetail deer ambling through the fields. But the question of the bats lingered, even after I returned home to Baltimore. Why didn't they come? Their absence felt like an abandonment.

I didn't even consider that the bats had dwindled in numbers, but a Google search proved Occam's razor: I didn't see the bats because they no longer existed. They were now endangered with over 90% having succumbed to white-nose syndrome, a fatal pathogen that struck the region around 2008 (when I was mothering a two-year-old and trying to hold onto my first marriage). That the answer to the question of the bats is so quantifiable galled me. There was no room for magical thinking. The bats are not, after all, about me.

I wanted to see the bats the way I wanted to see my dead friend, the way I wanted to see my younger self and tell her what I've learned, but the world carries on indifferently; nothing is static. In 2023 I mourned the bats with fresh grief, the kind of pain I felt when the phone rang in 2003, and I heard Flynn's father's voice, and my knees gave, and the whole house shook with my sobs. I wanted time to slow down, to let me catch my breath.

Only death preserves us. Flynn will remain a 26-year-old in plaid flannel with his sheepish grin, but those of us who are still alive will become unrecognizable even to ourselves. I don't know whether to count it as a blessing or a curse that this knowledge doesn't curb my longing to go back, even for just one evening. I could sit with that girl dangling her legs over the edge of the porch, Flynn's ghost beside us, courting infinite bats that swarmed the night.

The Last

Rebecca Hart Olander

In a board game we play, the person who goes first
is the last one to have ridden a train. The last train
I took was between Cambridge and Leominster,
where I'd left my car so Jerica and I could ride together
to the red-carpet Oscars-themed cancer benefit.

At a table of survivors, I was her escort. She'd done
my makeup for the last time, and we'd gotten ready
as girlfriends do, peeing with the door open,
pulling on stockings over our rolls, not caring if we saw.
That wasn't the last time I saw all of her. That was later,

in the January hospital. Between making a game
of the circular ward for her small son, placing the straw
between her cracked lips for diminishing sips of water,
and wiping her exposed brow, what were her last words?
And, mine to her? Did I take the time to tell her

how much I loved her and why, in case she wasn't already
carrying that with her, wherever she was going?

half-bath

Stephanie Anderson

in my head, the bathroom is red
velvet, soft synthetic curtains
mossed onto the wall. the sink
is dark, brassy fixtures, tall
antique mirror glossed

with some reflection
of a narrow half-bath, i've decided,
dimly lit and ornate. this is how
it happens in my head, that you

lean your forehead on the sink
for support but keep bending,
bending to the tiles, cool against
your skin, dark blue or black, maybe

gilded grout work. i want it to be gilded
when they find you, curled
against the floor, soft palm
prints in the wall, crack of dawn

glinting in the mirror. actually,
i want them not to find you.
i want you to have rested
for a moment, stood, dried

your hands and left, nothing
taken, moved into the next day.
in my head, we meet much later,
visit old photographs and remark

how young you look
compared to now.

Prelude

Jennifer Randall Hotz

I think it'll be a routine ultrasound.

"Measuring a little big," the doctor says.
I think: maybe linebacker?
I think: probably tall?
I think: possibly C-section?

After the exam,
left alone in the room,
I stare at the acoustic ceiling tiles
for over twenty minutes,

try to make out
constellations, then spot
a picture of a barred owl
looking straight at me.

The tech returns with a doctor:
"Take a picture of that aorta.
Now that one."
Both leave the room,
say nothing.

I note: neither doctor nor tech
look me in the eyes.
I feel the air shift as
the owl spreads its wings.

My husband is the one to tell me:
first about the twins part.
I start to tease him:

"You always wanted more
kids than I did . . ."
but he stops me:
"They are conjoined."

My cry:
keening in a voice not my own.

The owl lifts off,
wimples the atmosphere,
fixes its gaze on its prey.

Intake Form After the 2024 Election

Hillary Smith-Maddern

Have there been changes in your normal routine?
Define changes. Define normal. Define routine. I drink
more than I used to. I sleep sometimes
less, sometimes more. Conversations like stripped
wires unravel, sparks catch
between ghosts and unexploded landmines.
On a scale of 1–10, I'd say I ricochet between
moral panics and something lusher,
this scarlet letter smudged unwashable
on the back of my hand. Drink with me,
today's unhinged.

How often do you experience anxiety or depression?
This morning, instead of grappling with reality,
I recited the lyrics to "One Day More" from *Les Mis*,
like a manic prayer. My pipe dream is to cage dive
in dark, chummy waters, breath fogging
my mask as I face the jagged
grins of frenzied great whites. I swipe right on fear,
and I'm getting too old to play Éponine.

How often do you feel hopeless about the future?
I am chronically underprepared for battle,
stymied on a sagging jungle gym,
armed only with a choir preaching back at me
and a bottle of Chablis, gone warm in my hand.
The coup is always in the next room,
its boots shuffling like late night static.
But I keep vigil, drunk on the buzz and
the cannons. Good luck with the ramparts.

Southern Summer #5
Keri Withington

I drive by the river, AC blasting against
summer heat; history podcast blasting over
traffic noise. Rowers melt into the horizon.

The hosts talk about Oppenheimer.
There's a hole in the skyline; towers
demolished before a July dawn.

We blow up our lives when
it's too painful not to;
lawsuits over the old

coal plant, carcinogens in the playground. Panic attacks. Who are we when
we don't recognize ourselves in the

mirror? How do we know where we are when our land-
marks are rubble? The sound of your blood whooshing. The
lifeblood of Appalachia dammed, boiled for steam, your

heartbeat distant. The bomb was built here
when they thought it would scare everyone
into world peace. We self-regulate

to the sound of water.
Construction starts on the
nuclear plant here soon.

In Sharp Relief

Audrey J. Whitson

It was you who taught me how to see negative space.
When we watched films together you said to look behind the
foreground, beyond the characters and the dialogue; focus on
the backdrop. Study the wallpaper, the paintings, the ceiling
fixtures, the mouldings, the furniture. Study the scene out a
window, the books on the shelf, the music playing. I still do it
myself when I watch a film. So many clues to a story hidden in
plain view. Like our marriage. Sometimes I was so caught up
in what was going on around us, I could ignore what was going
on between us.

That's how I like to remember our three weeks in London:
all backdrop. For the longest time afterward, I told people it was
five weeks. We did so much, saw so much. It wasn't my first trip
to the city, but it felt that way with you as my guide. Like looking
through a kaleidoscope: scenes spliced, patterns changing with
each turn, every streetscape a new world, the view rich, vivid,
bold.

It was November but the weather unseasonably warm, almost
balmy. Warm southwesterlies were coming off the coast of Africa,
blowing through our flat, smelling of sea when the tide came up
the Thames.

With Christmas approaching, all the stores had
custom window displays: storied costumed figures, coloured
lights, and window dressings of snow. Just to walk in the door
of Fortnum & Mason transported me. Counters piled high
with boxed Turkish delight (lemon and apple blossom), fudges,
chocolates, and candied apples and apricots and every other
conceivable fruit. Marzipan in the shape of quinces, strawberries,
pears, peaches, oranges, and lemons. Old-fashioned candy. Ice
cream in dozens of flavours. Pastries. Preserves both savoury and
sweet. Tins of tea stacked high. You had to pull me away.

Liberty's of London's four storeys were like walking through the decks of an old ship. On the third floor, bolts of cloth lined the walls: cottons, linens, and silks from the four corners of the earth. I wanted to look at everything and took hours deciding. The cotton squares for scarves started at £50 GBP. The silk ones started at £90 GBP. My lifelong love of textiles sated by just standing in that place, I bought one of each.

London's streets held the ghosts of so many for me, some fictional, some real. Virginia Woolf walking across Gordon Square, Mrs. Dalloway making her way over Regent's Park to the florist. The Bloomsbury Group in residence on Russell. All the squares: Bedford, Gordon, Berkeley, Tavistock. All the parks: Hyde, Green, St. James. On Hampstead Heath, I kept seeing John Keats as I imagined him, dressed in a white shirt with puffy sleeves, riding pants, boots, long hair flung back, laughing, holding hands with a woman he loved, or perhaps just regarding her like a jewel. Was this Fanny Brawne in my mind? It was years before I would see *Bright Star*; the resemblance to that original apparition, eerie. We visited George Orwell's house down the hill. Then the gravestone of Douglas Adams in Highgate Cemetery dressed with quirky offerings. We made the long trek on the Tube and then by the Overground to Kew Gardens, where slips and saplings from the whole inhabited world are in residence.

You were 15 the first time you saw London, on a band trip from the Canadian prairies; it opened the world to you. A world you wanted to share with me decades later. I marvelled at your knowledge of each passage, lane, corner, and plaque. Gough Square, where Samuel Johnson wrote his dictionary. Over there, the Westminster Abbey Chapter House and the origins of Parliament. Here, the Inns of Court: the Inner Temple, Temple Church, Middle Temple, Fountain Court, and just inside the Inner Temple Gateway where we sat one day and you regaled me with a history of habeas corpus and common law. Why you loved the law so much. How the law was like a sacred text with its own rituals, protocols, and honours. A perfect order. Public service, your calling.

In you I had a superb guide to all the movements of art since the Renaissance: from the National Gallery to the Tate Modern. The Victoria and Albert, your favourite museum, chock full of fashion and design through the centuries. The tearooms fitted out by the designers of their day: William Morris, a revelation for me. Every street of the city a showcase for Western architecture before and after the Great Fire.

These positive impressions fill my journal entries, but there were outliers on the page, notes in the margin, digressions where the setting is no longer a character, we are no longer onlookers but subjects of our own drama.

In the lead-up to our 10th wedding anniversary that year, you wanted to throw a party, book a hall, a band, invite friends and family. You wanted to celebrate! I hid behind custom; I said it wasn't done. People don't have parties for their 10th wedding anniversary. They go off and have a quiet dinner by themselves somewhere. I wouldn't admit it to you, but I didn't want to fete our relationship that year, a year of conflict and divergence. I kept thinking things would get better in five, 10, 15 years' time; we would come through this, be better for it.

But what is not said fell like a shadow over our trip to London. The day you took me to the night market on Tottenham Court Road. We'd just come off the bus on The Strand and were making our way north. "This way," you said. Past Trafalgar Square, onto Charing Cross Road. "There's a good secondhand bookstore just along here." A myriad of bookshops. Marchpane, then Foyles. Everything from the popular to the arcane. "The market's near here. I know it," you said. And we rushed on. Past ratty storefronts, restaurants, theatres, the nighttime blur of crowds, bright fluorescents, hawkers selling CDs, traffic honking. At the top of Oxford and Charing Cross Road, a group of Roma played jazz with an accordion, trumpet, and bongos. They were lively, fresh. I wanted to linger, but you pulled me along.

"It's here," you said.

"Where?"

"Up ahead."

Some blocks on, we reached the makeshift market, blue tarp flung over booths. You searched for a familiar sign above all the rest. Electronics. "Here it is." You were happy, excited even, finding the market 20 years later exactly where you had left it. "They have the best prices," you said. A display of laptops, mobiles, radios. This time you've come to buy a small portable transistor radio for our stay. "They were fair to me," you said. It seemed an exchange of sorts, a settling of debts. I wasn't sure yet of the context.

But after the purchase you sat down on a bench and pounded your heart with your fist. Twenty years on, grief rolled over you, the words poured forth. How, at the same booth, you'd had to pawn a rare Japanese laptop for the fare home. You had told your then wife things were going well, you were almost done with your thesis, and you were coming home a few weeks early. That's when she ended it, without warning. Cancelled your joint credit cards, closed your bank account, walked away with everything. How you'd found out she was gone. Divorce was the one time the law was your enemy, was not orderly, could not be counted on. I'd heard the story in bits and pieces over the course of our marriage but never with such force and comprehension.

There was a quiet green space tucked behind St. Clement Danes, the bells ringing a medley called the London Surprise Royal. Most days just after six in the evening, they rang for a good half hour. "The Angelus," someone said. Sometimes we could hear them from our flat. One day we were walking by as they started to play, and we sat in the churchyard, just the two of us, and listened till they ended.

Almost every day we attended a noon-hour concert in a place of worship, sometimes evensong or vespers. That's when you told me the music in the churches kept you going during that dark time, both for warmth and solace. The churches, museums, libraries, galleries, all free or by donation. And there, under the bridges and the overpasses we walked by, were the benches you'd slept on, taken shelter. How you'd had to sell off your suits one by one to keep body and soul together.

When I look at my journal from those weeks, I see our story in the foreground. A study of miscommunication. We fought over petty things. Where to hang the towels in the bathroom. What gifts to buy our friends. We misheard each other's simplest desires: to attend or to leave this lecture, try this restaurant, or catch that train.

A study of tensions. I wrote that I had racoon eyes from waking often. Once, from a dream, gasping for breath: I was in a gallery but couldn't find my way out. It was like an excavation, tunnels of grey rock. I couldn't breathe there. This marriage. Our relationship. Your grief.

A study of marital collapse. You were exhausted, you said, the word you used for pain. You felt hollow, you said, the word you used for depression. What I didn't see then was that you were exhausted from being together, but you didn't want to be apart either. You needed a break, but you wouldn't let me explore without you. Maybe this was how you felt in our day-to-day relationship, too? And so, in the evenings you drank.

We fought about your drinking: the obligatory visit to the pub for "a pint or two" of Guinness, the proscriptive vodka before bed and during the night, the attempts to hide the bottles. The sex that was laboured, joyless. You grew more exhausted, testy, shouting at me in the theatre, at the Tube station, the museum. The criticism mounted, the sarcasm on both sides.

"You're sad," you observed one morning. I was sad. "I want us to be close," you kept saying. You thought this trip would bring us together. "But you're cold," you told me. Cold of feeling. Maybe I was cold. You wanted me to take care of you, I know now. But I had stopped being that wife.

Maybe that explains how you ended it a year after our journey to London. Only this time it is me coming from the bus, alone, rushing along the streets, finally sitting, overcome at our end. Your announcement came over supper where we were staying during an insurance loss, a rental: all the furniture, the appliances, the electronics done up in black. The place cavernous even for two. You were freshly showered, clothes changed. You waited till we had eaten, exchanged news of the day. Only then, when you told me you were going home without me, did I see the foreground and the background separating, the edges of the shot blurring. Our marriage in sharp relief.

Days before the end, you told me the truth about our aborted 10th wedding anniversary. You weren't fooled at all by my appeal to convention. You told me how much it had hurt, that negation of our marriage. Irreversible. Our relationship a place of yearning, but not a place of refuge for either of us. This lack. This sorrow at wanting. You were braver than me in saying that it was over. That it felt lonelier in the marriage than out of it. At some level it was an honest reckoning; I had been leaving the marriage for a long time.

I forgive you. Please forgive me.

In Defense of Career Suicide

erica r. such

my best friend was in her second year of veterinary school
working at the volunteer wildlife clinic
when a man with an Iowa driver's license
brought in a vulture.

he said the bird was flailing
alongside a highway exit lined
with burdock, its feathers sticking
to the blood scratched into the asphalt.

three bullet holes seeped out
more dark liquid when she dug
her fingers around the shards
of copper & powder to pry
out the buckshots forming
a triangle on its right wing.

it was the first time an animal refused to die.
it ate the *rage against the dying of the light*
for it knew suffering

was what carried itself on our Earth's plane
gliding on the winds of epinephrine & cortisol
desperate to catch a flight
it would never lose

& when my dearest friend
who wore all black when
her hissing cockroach passed away
posed the anesthesia mask to its small face
& pressed phenobarbital into its chest

the vulture floated gently
into that good night of absolute
nothingness, the bird finally killed only
when it had been relieved of its torment.

whatever a spirit burns itself into
when the body can no longer keep it
passed from the vulture & into her
& as she begged to no longer be
a veterinarian,
i no longer wanted to be
a poet.

how my desire to trace
the romantic justice of predators
dying as prey, to take tragedy & feast
on its carrion as it decays
in the eloquent acid
of my stomach
was not for compassion
or the bitter pursuit of beauty

but animalistic instinct to transform
the cruel poetry of life
into an illustrious career that would keep me
alive even when the agony of consumption
blows me away into a lush oblivion

of parasitic bows & applause,
wearing someone else's
bloodied feathers, pretending i know
what it's like to lose
the ability to fly when i am the one

staring down the barrel of a gun
aimed at the poet
in the mirror with waxing wings
who didn't know
she was going to die either way.

A poet died today

Amy Devine

and my pay did not come through in time to
cover the rent and the car and the child's fresh
blueberries, still wet in the punnet.

The poet lived on a mountain, and I live
in mouldy brick, but we both woke with something
growing in our lungs, and that counts as family.

Someone dressed in blue gingham told me
that this waiting is not the same as wanting
things to change, and I agree; it is so much worse.
I want to birth something worthy of mountains,
of the ripest fruit, of the first thought in your mind when
you see frangipanis in the wet season.
I emerged from a bloodline of starving artists
and housewives and still this month is the deepest thing
that I have ever swum through.

The poet was not somebody that I knew,
but they knew me, in the way that all poets do.
Tomorrow there will be enough for the cat food,
for the talcum powder, for the Diet Coke cold in the fridge.

Blue Jacket

Kathleen Weed

Unseasonably warm for June in San Francisco
—a month where we locals shake our heads
at shivering tourists in T-shirts and Bermuda shorts.
Joe DiMaggio Playground. A birthday celebration.
My grandson turning three.

Bubbles, balloons, party bags, a Curious
George slice of cake for any child who that day
happened by. Bob's Donuts and Peet's Coffee, too,
for weary moms and nannies—compliments
of my son's wife.

I planned for fog.
I wore my daughter's faded denim jacket.
Not a jacket day. I took it off.
I took it off, and somebody took it.

There's a photo of me still wearing it.
I'm popping bubbles with the birthday boy.
The fabric patterned. Lots of daisies.
Simple stemless petals, white and yellow
perfect circles, bling-pink stamens
round as summer baseballs—

Most like a child's doodle.
A child who might cry out,
Come see my picture, Mama.
And you'd leave, for a moment,
your magazine, a nodding glance,
a smile sufficing praise. A Gap
jean jacket my daughter bought
twenty-something years ago.

She's been dead a quarter century.
So longer than that.

My daughter-in-law remembered—
was more upset than I was. She made
a poster, offered a reward. She was
more upset than I let on that I was.

It had felt good to see that jacket hanging
in my closet, a go-to topcoat I turned to
more often than not, although I long
ago had stopped myself believing
it might conjure the faint ghost
flesh of my daughter's bare shoulders
touching mine.

Still, my daughter-in-law's distress
on my account unlatched my muzzled
mother-mind, granting me a glancing
clemency—leave to miss my daughter
missing her little nephew's party.
My usual knack for swallowing
that sharp grief rock—a feat honed
slick as a magician eating fire—
for once not needed.

It was a blue-sky day. A blue sky flecked
with iridescent bubbles. Rainbow orbs floating
evanescent, like I could imagine an unexpected
kindness might do. How fragile they were.
Wet, airborne bubbles, like bursting
kisses that found me teeter-tottering
beneath blue sky, a toddler's sturdy body
warming my lap. A day where I was mostly
happy—I lost a jacket. We ate cake.

Miscarriage, November 6, 2024

Patricia Davis-Muffett

On the day after the accident,
once my body assessed the damage,
things were quiet.

No words to say. No experts
to call. I stood in the living room,
bleeding, grieving. No crystal ball
to show me the life that waited—
focused instead on ordering chaos.
I pulled every book from the shelves—
piles on the splintered hardwood:
poetry, fiction, nonfiction,
A to C, D to F, and so on.
Sorting for hours, I stopped only
to change the pads I bled through,
wipe snot from my face.

This morning, I rise in the dark,
make coffee, survey the chaos.
I will wash these dishes.
I will throw away these rotting
vegetables. I will wipe the counters
and take out the trash. I will make a plan
to feed my family, fill my kitchen counter
with those I love, and gather strength
for what comes next.

Under the Siren: Alexandria, 1973

Johanna Elattar

A photograph shows me at three years old, seated before a cake on a pedestal, flowers arranged like sentries at the edge of the frame. I wear a white lace dress that scratches my collarbone and a veil pinned into the heavy part of my long, dark hair. My eyes are lowered, solemn, as if I understood the weight of the moment. But the truth is simpler: I had a fever, my eyes watered constantly, and the photographer's lights were too sharp for me to face. "Look down at the cake," he instructed, and I obeyed. No child looked more serious than I did in that picture.

It was October 1973 in Alexandria, Egypt, and the city was at war. My parents had braved the blackout, the barricades, and the fear to bring me to that photography studio because they wanted proof—a record that their daughter had a birthday, even under the siren.

At three years old, I was already fluent in the language of danger. The "danger siren," as my mother called it, wailed its orders: lights off, voices low, tar paper sealed to the windows. Outside our building, a red brick barricade cut the street short, an abrupt wall in the middle of everyday life.

I knew the rules even then. Don't touch toys left in the street; they might be traps disguised as playthings. Don't stand near the window. Don't wander past the barricade. Adults whispered these warnings not to frighten us but to keep us alive. Years later, someone scoffed when I told the story. "No such bombs existed," he said. "That's just village gossip." But he hadn't been there. I had. And I hadn't lived in a village. I lived in Alexandria, a city with a library that once held the world. In a season of danger, rules that protect small hands are not myths. They are survival.

I was sick the night the photograph was taken, chest rattling, eyes watering, but I wanted the celebration. No friends came—it was too dangerous. Instead, the grown-ups filled the room: my grandparents, aunts with bracelets sliding down their wrists, uncles with their jokes, and my parents arranging the cake as if arranging a fragile world. My grandmother had chosen the dress I wore; my mother had smoothed my hair with oil, and the veil was her idea—a small act of sweetness inspired by my parents' wedding photograph.

The candles were lit on the cake, and everyone leaned close. They sang "Happy Birthday" in hushed voices, the melody pressed down until it barely floated above the table. When I blew the candles out, they raised their hands and mimed applause, palms meeting the air but never each other. Silent clapping, joy without noise. I looked at their faces and thought, *You can clap with a smile.* That night I learned it was true.

What I remember most are sensations. The smell of sugar icing mixing with the chemical bite of tar paper. The heat of the candles turning into halos through my watery eyes. The weight of the veil tugging on my scalp where my mother had pinned it too tight. My grandmother's hand on my shoulder, steady, rhythmic—one, two, three—as if counting to help anchor me to the room. My father at the window, two fingers slipping into the seam, listening to the city more than looking at it.

I don't remember the words the adults said that night. I remember the quiet choreography of protection. A hand smoothing hair. A match striking. A song sung carefully. A smile that took the place of clapping.

That photograph has followed me through the decades, but even without it I would remember. Some memories lodge themselves so deeply they never leave. I've been carrying that night with me for 51 years. I've thought of it during other storms in my life, whenever the world felt unsafe or when voices around me said, "Be small, be silent, don't be seen."

The siren taught me silence. But the cake, the song, the mimed applause—they taught me something stronger. Joy doesn't need permission. It can whisper and still survive.

When I think of that night, I sometimes think of Anne Frank
in the annex—writing about a jar of jam, a string of beads, or a
chestnut tree glimpsed through a window. She recorded not only
fear but the small joys that made survival human. Her story has
always felt close to me, not only because of its universal truth but
because my own mother—Muslim—carried Jewish roots in her
family history. Anne Frank is not distant from me; she threads
through my bloodline.

That connection reminds me that no matter the era, no
matter the war, families insist on memory. They record birthdays,
they sing softly, they protect joy, because they know children will
carry those moments forward long after the sirens stop.

And so I cannot forget, as I write this, that children in
Gaza today are also blowing out candles in blackouts. Mothers
there are also smoothing their children's hair in the dark. Families
are also whispering lullabies and miming clapping so that joy
does not alert danger. Those children will carry these moments,
too—not as statistics or politics but as memories of how love
refuses to vanish. Fifty years from now, they will remember, just
as I do.

The photograph from October 1973 shows a solemn child in
lace, eyes lowered toward a cake, flowers arranged around her. It
does not show the barricade waiting outside, the tar paper over
the windows, or the warnings about toys. It does not capture the
sound of hushed voices singing or the sight of silent clapping.

But I remember. I remember perfectly.

That is what it meant to live under the siren.

Right On Time

Katharine Weinmann

After sharing the spring-themed luncheon you'd prepared
in celebration of my Aries birthday, you asked me
how it felt turning seventy.

Ours is a long-time friendship, kindled in asanas
practiced on yoga mats.
With years of soulful conversations in the sangha
of our making,
I counted on your question to evoke a considered response.
And so, I sat still and silent for several minutes, thinking

back to the candles on the café dessert
that I blew out earlier in the week. Not the chocolate cake
I would have hoped for, but a good enough opportunity
to make a wish. Not for me, but for my friend living with, or,
depending on the results of regular MRIs,
dying from a deadly cancer;

about my life, and all the right turns and wrong ones.
The wise choices I'd made, and the not-so-wise ones.
The balance sheet of regrets and reliefs.
Family and friends present for a reason, a season, a lifetime.
The grief and the grace in it all, and in what's still to come.

And without thinking,
deep from my belly,
out of my mouth,
burst the answer,
"I'm right on time."

And you burst out laughing
with the absolute rightness
of it all.

TIGERS
Kristin Camitta Zimet

Down the road a bankrupt neighbor's house
crawls with women out to clean the flesh
off the bones. Cupboards raked, closets torn
open, skins in a heap. You grit your teeth,
tasting the emptiness. Nothing is left
in Silvio's garage. In Alessa's kitchen,
sadness clings to surfaces like grease.

Nothing here, but—part of you that's six
stirs in the playroom. In the corner is
a den; tigers are purring at a pitch you
nearly hear. Glass eyes swivel, hackles rise;
a threadbare beast in you begins to whine,
some cub who knew where it belonged
before your husband died. These old toys

must manage to be loved, you think,
for the children's sake. Almost, you feel
a pounce. You sink onto the rug, shaking
your head. What would you do with them,
what will you do from now on with your own
stripped life? The tigers yawn. They lick
their lips. Solitude, they snarl. Unsafe.

They tell you, go hunt down the things
you need. Plush heads pivot; whiskers
point; you've sprung to your feet, gone
halfway down the hall. Is that your heart
or do you hear them panting heavily,
and when did you turn? Bumping buyers,
bungling past "Everything Must Go,"

clutching them, you leap at the cashier,
then to the street, tiger in your right arm,
tiger in the crook of your left arm,
tails dangling, your white hair flying.

Closures

Renee Emerson

They aim to make short work of it,
three branches lopped off.

"No budget for them," the board claims.
Shutter the doors on the teen book club;
Summer Reading Challenge; students
clustered at tables, putting their tutors
through their paces; abandoned
puzzles half-pieced together.

Let the geriatrics trace their lifelines
of genealogy elsewhere—
where is elsewhere? "It's all gone
digital," they say, "our patrons are changing
what they ask for, what they select."

In the story circle, the children are neighbors
who don't know each other's names.
Yet they still listen, still join hands.

Jill

Chelsea Yates

I met her through photocopied fliers scotch-taped to storefront windows.[1] The local radio station taught me how to pronounce her last name. The grown-ups I knew rarely said it out loud. When they did, they spoke it cautiously, as if doing so might summon a demon.

My friend Trent remembers her because she went missing the one summer his family drove to Nashville and visited the Grand Ole Opry. When they returned home, her disappearance was all over the news. The police came around to ask his parents if they'd seen anything suspicious in the neighborhood. His house had a McGruff the Crime Dog sign in their window, so a kid in trouble might've rung their bell. But, no, they'd been out of town.

She lived with her mom and brother in Kansas but had been spending the summer with her dad and stepmom in our little Nebraska town. They rented an apartment in a building near downtown, which at the time was a few blocks of wide parking and old buildings. I lived in a different part of town, but I was also aware of her disappearance. Everyone was. She was just nine, like Trent and me.

Her dad and stepmom worked early shifts and weren't home the morning it happened. She got herself up, dressed, and left the apartment. She walked to her babysitter's house, about three blocks from Trent's house. Instead of knocking on the front door or going around back, she sat on the front porch. That was the last anyone saw of her.

But kidnappings didn't happen in our town. At least, that's what everyone thought until hers. Our high school basketball team had won the state championship that spring with a last-second shot. Over the summer, there was a buzz in the air—the

---

1. This essay explores the disappearance of Jill Cutshall, a girl who went missing from Norfolk, Nebraska, in 1987, and has never been found.

kind of joy that makes a town feel invincible. Then, in August, her disappearance changed everything. The mood shifted. Something had taken flight that summer—not just her, but a sense of certainty, of safety, of what could and couldn't happen here.

Her parents were blamed. Broken home. Bad news. What was her dad thinking, leaving her alone at odd hours? Where was her stepmom? Not a suitable arrangement for kids, people said—as if poor judgment explained everything.

In the weeks, months, and eventually years that followed, her disappearance was treated less as a community tragedy and more as a family problem. Something unfortunate, yes—but it wasn't ours to worry about.

Maybe that was the story adults told us kids so we wouldn't be scared. Or maybe it was what they told themselves so they wouldn't be. But the truth was simpler, and more terrifying: it could have happened to any of us.

****

Her disappearance loomed over the start of fourth grade. Her mom moved to town to be closer to the search. "MISSING" posters filled bulletin boards and shop windows. Some featured a hand-drawn illustration of her, which surprised some of us kids who thought only cops on TV shows worked with sketch artists on that kind of thing. Others presented what looked like a photocopied school picture. I remember thinking the two images didn't look much alike.

I liked her smile from the photograph, though. It was bright, and she had big front teeth—the kind that must have recently grown in, replacing baby teeth. Her long blonde hair was parted in the middle, each side pulled back in a barrette. I'd stare at her likeness, curious if we'd been at the swimming pool together or gone down the tornado slide at the park, one after the other. I wondered what her favorite cereal was and what Saturday morning cartoons she liked best.

Here's something I don't remember: changes. We kids still walked to school unattended and returned to empty houses in the afternoon. We played in our front yards and rode our bikes around town unsupervised. We were instructed not to talk to strangers or get into strange cars—as if we would have had control in those situations.

****

The T-shirt, jeans, and underwear she'd been wearing were found about three months later, on the grounds of a nearby wildlife refuge. Eventually, two men were accused of abducting her. Both lived in the same apartment building as her dad and stepmom. Both had records. Both were questioned. Neither was arrested. A few years later, her mom petitioned signatures to convene a grand jury, which determined there was sufficient evidence to bring one of the men to trial. He was convicted of kidnapping and sentenced to life in prison. The other was not charged.

There was never a confession, or a body.

****

Trent and I didn't know each other the summer she went missing. We became friends one afternoon a few years later sitting side by side during a junior high assembly. For years, our friendship fluttered like moths around a porch light, drawn to shared curiosities. We traded favorite songs and poets, ate school lunches together, and later, in college, found ourselves in the same classrooms with the same professors. Now, in our mid-40s, we still circle each other's sky, making a point to check in, to stay tethered.

We never spoke of her back then, when we first met in junior high, though in our own ways we both carried her with us. It wasn't until a recent catch-up call that she surfaced between us. We talked about the trace she left behind—the unsettled questions and the thoughts that still unsettle us. Her

65

disappearance taught us that bad things don't always come with a reason, or a warning. Sometimes they just happen.

****

But I like to think she flew. That morning, the moment she turned away from the babysitter's front door, I imagine she sprouted small wings—fragile, trembling, but determined. As she fought and thrashed and screamed, those wings caught fire. Fueled by fury, they grew stronger, brighter, until she broke away, rising in a blaze that scorched the hands that tried to hold her down.

And then she hovered above them, above us—no longer just a little girl, but something more: a beautiful bird reborn in flame, wings now fully feathered and glowing, trailing embers, free to catch the sunlight.

At the post office
Giulia Paglione

[A276]
And the stamps behind the glass
Look like miniature paintings in a museum
[A277]
The grey marble floor
The nasal sound of a printer
A woman sitting next to me is tapping her feet impatiently

[A278] [A279] [A280]
I try not to stare at the screen that says A281
Or at my ticket that screams A294
[A282] [A283] [A284]

The traffic noise from the street
In the early evening
[A285] [A286] [A287]

You have already received my letter
If there was love, I think I hid it well
Did you hide yours

[A288] [A289] [A290]
That inexplicable inescapable string of events
That brought me here today
And brought you there that day
[A291] [A292] [A293]

A294 in my shaking hands
And the postwoman disappears behind the front desk
"Ypograpste edo, to onoma sas, efcharisto"
And she hands me the yellow envelope with a smile

My feet take me to Syntagma Square
Where I sit under a tangerine tree
The car horns explode
The protesters scream at the police
But there's only you, the tangerines, and me

On Seeing Jack Whitten's Painting, 9.11.01

Aileen Bassis

The unbearable
detritus of a city
accumulated
on a wall before me.

Vast expanse of tiny
bits—footprints
pieces pressed
from sidewalks
and sewer grates
blood and ashes
bone and newsprint.

Meaning severed
from broken moments—
into a present larger
than any one.

My tears surprised me
with a memory

      (the bereft fall and empty
      spring when my neighbor said
      she was lucky because they found
      her husband's wedding ring
      in the towers' rubble).

I stood silenced before her loss
our budding hedges lined
with heedless daffodils
multiplying year after year

but here before this assemblage
of shiny bits glimmering
among opaque painted squares
I'm unexpectedly reminded
that we're fragile in our random
accident of time and need to find
a way across this, our continent
of grief.

Still Here, Still Breathing
Deepti Bhatia

After the Bhopal Gas Tragedy, December 1984

That night,

the sky turned into a wound.

No sirens.

Just coughing.

Just eyes burning in the dark.

My mother says

she ran with me wrapped in a shawl

soaked in milk;

someone told her it would help,

but nothing helped.

Behind us,

people fell like chopped wheat,

clutching throats,

their lungs turning against them.

They called it methyl isocyanate,

We called it death.

Air gone wrong.

The factory, Union Carbide,

left its breath in our bodies.

But this is not a poem about that night.

This is about the days after.

The years.

The decades.

This is about children
born with twisted limbs,
spines like question marks,
asking why.
About women
who stopped bleeding
at twenty-two.
About boys
who never learned to run
without gasping.
The factory still stands,
rusted, hollow, fenced,
but the poison didn't stay inside.
It slid into the groundwater,
whispered into wombs,
made a home in our bones.
Compensation came
in envelopes too thin,
never enough for surgeries,
never enough for justice.
Sometimes journalists come.
They take pictures of the old signboard,
of a woman with a missing eye,
of a child too quiet.
Then they leave.
But we remain,
still breathing in Bhopal.

Still holding our protest posters
next to our medical bills.
Still marching with lungs
that rattle in the winter.
And yet,
there is resistance in our breath.
In the women who teach disabled children
how to paint joy with crooked fingers.
In the youth who turn the poison site
into a mural of memory.
In the lawyers
who speak the names of the dead
like mantras in courtrooms.
We live,
not because the world fixed us
but because we refused to vanish.
In the place
where the air once betrayed us,
we are planting trees,
not because we forgot,
but because we remember
everything.
And we are still here.
Still here.
Still breathing.

Quilting
Vivian Walman-Randall

I learned to sew	in my grandmother's	home office
upstairs	guest bedroom, there are	sewing machines
I tucked the quilt in	bureau drawers	in a place far from
my mother's closet	where quilts are kept from	an aunt who
gave a piece of history before	my great aunt	dies in a car crash
our threads are tied,	a sister	is stitched and tucked away
my aunt smiles—my sister	is named for her	my daughter
is wrapped in a quilt	decades later	named after my sister

Some Promises Were Meant to be Broken

Cam McGlynn

For Mom

I swore to never leave you,
back when promises held the weight
of a raindrop
running off the back of a duck.
I marked the distance
between here and there
and I promised to always
stay.

Here
is a good land
to grow up in. Lemonade stands
and fireflies. Sandboxes.
Oatmeal cream pies.
Sprinklers and pillow forts.
Here
is the endless summer
of puddles and popsicles.
Here
is the eight o'clock bedtime.
Here
is Thanksgiving dinner set for twelve.

There
is a world far beyond.
Concert tickets
and road trips. All-nighters.
Bonfires
and dorm rooms.
Double espresso shots.

There
is the overstuffed van
on move-in day.
There
is sliding down icy hilltops
on stolen cafeteria trays.
There
is the meteor shower
reflecting over the river.

I would promise
to never leave you,

but I think I'm already gone.

Meet Me at Burning Man

Danielle Salerno

"We should go to Burning Man *together*!" Your eyes are wide and bright with possibility. Or maybe that's the mushrooms you got from your crush-du-jour—the CrossFit fanatic who's volunteering with maintenance this week. My own memory of the summer I spent volunteering at a Buddhist retreat center is hazy from a cocktail of fresh grief and pilfered bourbon. When I think back on that summer evening, what I remember most is the promise of a future that peeks through our inebriation.

This night is a colorful one—psychedelic orange peals of laughter swirl through the closed book-and-gift store where we take shelter, avoiding the damp cold of the staff quarters, flimsy canvas platform tents that were freezing at night and sweltering during the day, for just a few hours more. The sound of our hilarity slips between gossamer shreds of pastel-hued tulle as we gleefully tear long, thin strips of lilac and lavender from the crumpled mass of fabric on the floor at our feet, then knot them to the band of white elastic around your waist.

I can see my distorted reflection staring back at me with bleary eyes from the holographic lenses of the oversized ski goggles you wear on your forehead, as you model the epic thrift-store find that you picked up in Fort Collins that morning. It hasn't yet occurred to either of us that if ski goggles are deemed a necessary accessory to protect the eyes from the desert sun and sand, perhaps it would be wise to go to Nevada wearing more than a handmade tutu and body paint. But tonight is not meant for wisdom. Tonight we dream and plan for a future we know won't arrive; a truth we both studiously ignore.

Here in this bubble, time is elastic. In the span of two short months, I've made a best friend. It's a friendship with a predetermined end date. The flames of Burning Man are visible on our horizon, yet they're just as inaccessible to me as

you'll be two weeks from now, when I'm scheduled to leave
this mountaintop Shambhala and reenter reality. We don't
acknowledge it. Sometimes I wish you would, if only so that I can
be sure that you think about it as much as I do; that I'll be missed
by more than the deer and the mullein.

Maybe it's an effect of the rarefied mountain air, but
everything here is fast and deep and intense. Smells, sounds,
emotions, and friendships are accelerated and magnified, often
leaving me dizzy and nauseated in a way that was easy at first to
mistake for altitude sickness before I knew better.

When I arrived in Colorado two months ago, fleeing both
a confrontation with mortality and my father's untimely new
girlfriend, acquired only a month after my mother's sudden
passing, it was with the kind of all-consuming sense of FOMO
that can only come from locking eyes with the Grim Reaper. Such
a painful reminder of the inevitability of death lit an existential
fire under my ass. I thirsted for adventure even as I drank from
the cup of grief.

That's how you drew me in. Loud, colorful, and steeped in
drama of your own making, you're anything but boring. Perhaps
you're the type of friend that would be exhausting in the day-to-
day banality of my previous corporate existence—but here in this
liminal space where there's nothing to do beyond meditate, cry,
and pull invasive species out of the cracked dirt by their roots,
you are the water that slakes my thirst. It is impossible to have
FOMO around your colorful chaos.

Which is how we became fast friends, and how I find myself
perched on a meditation cushion in the middle of the spiritual
book-and-gift store you manage at 1 a.m., constructing a
costume for a festival I know I won't get to see. You have an easy
persuasiveness about you. I almost believe we'll be there, together.
Tonight, I want to believe.

There are so many things I want to say to you but don't,
despite knowing I'll likely never see you again. There's no cell

service here in the middle of the forested mountains of Colorado, and you "don't believe in social media." You're a professional nomad, and when we both leave this place, there will be no practical way to keep in contact. Perhaps we could be pen pals, but we won't write. I'll be too busy with the mind-numbing minutia of an office job, and you'll be tripping in the desert in your purple tutu.

So I never thank you for surrounding me with your protective cloud of vitality, which I was so desperate to find when I ran away from my whole life and drove myself across nine states to live in the middle of nowhere for the summer. All my friends and family thought I was crazy, so it was a comfort to not have to be the crazy one around you.

I never voice my gratitude to you for opening my heart to possibilities I'd never considered, and for opening my world to everything it could be when I stop confining myself to what should be—for helping me realize my mother's expectations for me were her own, and my bonds of obligation to them released upon her death. I was so scared of the blank page my life had suddenly become, and your unassuming friendship cured my writer's block. Your example showed me how empowering it can be to write my own story.

Of course, I never went to Burning Man with you. I don't even know if you ever made it there, but I hope you did. I hope you danced in the light of the pyre, flames reflecting in the holographic lenses of your fabulous ski goggles.

I hope wherever you landed was soft, that you surrounded yourself with friends that weren't afraid to tell you what you meant to them.

I hope you still have that faded purple tutu, that you trot it out from the far reaches of your closet every now and then to show your people. I hope you tell them the story of the night it was made.

At the Community Garden, We Talk of Root Systems

Pratibha Kumari Gupta

The woman with the sunflower tattoo
tells me about rhizomes,
how some things spread secretly underground,
sending up green shoots where you least expect.
How connection is not always a straight line
from branch to branch, but a tangled,
secret network beneath the surface.
We are knee-deep in soil and stories,
planting kale starts and the seeds of confessions.
She speaks of her son, his first year at college,
the quiet that has grown like a weed in his room.
I speak of my mother, her voice on the phone,
a thin thread I follow back home.
This plot of land is a quilt of our making,
each row a different stitch, a different history.
We water not just the plants, but the silence
between us, which is its own kind of language.
We are building a world from the ground up,
where the only requirement for membership
is the willingness to get your hands dirty,
to tend to the fragile, green hope of another.
Above us, the bees agree, moving
from blossom to blossom, making a map
of their own sweet, invisible connections.

On the Cover: The Awakening Aperture
Clara Garza

mixed-media collage

"The Awakening Aperture" was created as a mixed-media work that combines sewing supplies, suede cutouts, and layers of paper, torn in different ways for the effect of visible textures and irregular edges. This piece was captured using photography and digital formatting. The work connects to **KAIROS**—the right or opportune moment—with the black background suggesting continuous or ordinary time, and the circle interrupting it, calling attention to a decisive moment that stands apart. The circle (inspired by the aperture of a camera, or the lens that captures a fleeting fragment of time) is composed of pieces of the diary of a fictional college student experiencing college life, from the day she is accepted to the school to her graduation. Her initial doubt is reflected by the moody outer rim of the circle, and as she opens herself to the brightness of college, she starts to appreciate her life more fully.

Each paper fragment is a unique diary entry, documenting a brief moment in time—whether a momentous revelation, such as recognizing that she was no longer seeking permission to belong but had already become part of something larger than herself, or something simple, such as sitting in a library for the first time. The layering of the paper also reflects how moments are built from the accumulation of experiences, showing how even the smallest moments matter. Though each piece, each memory, is incomplete on its own, together they form a whole that symbolizes clarity and growth.

Reflections and Ponderings

Contributors were asked if they create through routine, or if they wait for their own kairos moment to find inspiration. Here are their thoughtful responses.

****

Stephanie Anderson, "half-bath"
"I've tried to have a routine. I would love to have a routine. Creatively, I don't think I can be anything consistently but restless. A few years ago, my regular writing regimen included keeping myself awake irresponsibly late; now I find my best work falls out of me in the 15 minutes before I am due to leave for somewhere. Everything I write ends up as part of a continual unwinding of my life and that's an ongoing stew masquerading as inspiration. Sometimes I have no choice but to write something immediately, but more often than not, it needs to simmer."

Aileen Bassis, "On Seeing Jack Whitten's Painting, *9.11.01*"
"I don't have a writing routine. I write when something moves me—it can be something I see, a phrase, a metaphor, or a feeling."

Deepti Bhatia, "Still Here, Still Breathing"
"There are days when I keep staring at the blank paper for hours; those are the moments of creative void and guilt. There also are times when my calm surfaces breach the normed boundaries, usually when I have feelings of retaliation, appreciation, or gratitude. During such times, triggered by the desire of conveyance, I write. So yes, my writings are attributed to certain special moments, when I let my feelings breathe in the open."

Loretta Cantieri, "The Second Abortion"
"I type daily pages but sometimes I do miss a date. If I am not generating new material, I revise poems. If inspiration comes and I am not in a position to write at that moment I will take notes on

paper or on my phone. Inspiration is an elusive critter, sort of like a lynx. It is wonderful if you have a sighting, but you may hike many days without seeing it."

Roxanne Christiana, "COLONIZING MARS"
"I create through routine: I start my writing sessions at 4:00 a.m. and continue to about 10:00 a.m. During that session I hope to get inspiration, which I usually do. Not always, though, in which case I'll write down my stream of consciousness and see if an idea emerges."

Virginia Ottley Craighill, "Last Poem for My Father"
"I have never been good at routine. I might be disciplined for a short time, but that discipline is usually disrupted by some unforeseen event that sends me in another direction. I've found that my kairos moment occurs when I am alone, or particularly when I'm out walking. In some ways, walking is a routine that frees the mind to become aware of patterns that break through the finite veil."

Patricia Davis-Muffett, "Miscarriage, November 6, 2024"
"I do my best to show up for my muse regularly, often in the morning, and try to give myself a little space and a push to write. Twice, I have done a 30/30 challenge, where I created and posted a new poem draft every day for 30 days. That experience taught me that I might be surprised at what is waiting if I stop and listen for a short period every day. My regular routine rarely gives me that kind of space every single day, but I do my best to give it space at least a few times a week."

Amy Devine, "A poet died today"
"I try to make a habit of creation, scheduling time to write or edit or read poetry on a regular basis. By doing this I give myself permission to take my art seriously, and I create space for inspiration to strike. That said, there is nothing like going about your day-to-day and suddenly witnessing or reading something

that has you desperately scrambling to write. I think that you need both the discipline and the inspiration to sustain creative work."

Johanna Elattar, "Under the Siren: Alexandria, 1973"
"I create through a combination of routine and kairos moments. I rely on consistent writing practices to develop ideas, but often inspiration strikes in unexpected, opportune moments that guide the direction of my work."

Renee Emerson, "Closures"
"I keep a set writing routine so that when the muse does come looking, she knows where to find me."

Clara Garza, "The Awakening Aperture"
"Although creation is one of the most important aspects of my life, I rely on patience and my own kairos to find inspiration. I understand that art cannot always be forced. Routine is consistent and reliable, but it is the decisive moment of vision that gives my work authenticity and meaning. In that sense, I create by honoring the moments when inspiration reveals itself."

Pratibha Kumari Gupta, "At the Community Garden, We Talk of Root Systems"
"I write through a modest routine of reading, reflection, and revision that keeps me close to language. Inspiration often arrives in moments of kairos—unexpected yet timely encounters that transform the routine into finished work. So my practice depends on both: steady rhythm and sudden revelation."

Taylor Harrison, "Fatherland"
"Even though I am very much a creature of habit, going as far as to schedule a few hours each weekend to force myself to write, I find both inspiration and the passion to create through my kairos moments. My favorite time to create is when inspiration strikes

and I am able to drive to a coffee shop and immediately get to work—those pieces seemingly write themselves."

Elizabeth Hazen, "Past Life"
"I am always trying to stick to a routine, but I think the more honest answer is that I create when inspiration hits. I try to write a little something every day, but my best work happens at times totally out of my own planning."

Jennifer Randall Hotz, "Prelude"
"I journal most mornings (usually no more than a page, sipping coffee, periodically staring out at the blossoming dawn) and try to dedicate blocks of time to creative work, but I also aim to be alert to emotions/images/phrases that might be the stirrings of a poem-in-waiting. More than once I've woken up in the middle of the night and hurried to jot down phrases before they flee."

Cam McGlynn, "Some Promises Were Meant to be Broken"
"I do both, but I'm a strong believer that you must put in the time and work for your inspiration to show up. I'm not much for actual 'routine' as a noun, in the sense of always writing at this time in this spot with this pen and notebook. But I do try to write 'routinely,' often and however I can—scribbling notes at the doctor's office, typing up a poem on my lunch break, poems beside grocery lists across dozens of different notebooks. . . . Both methods can result in a fire, but one is more reliable, if harder work, than the other. If I'm struggling to write, I remind myself what I need for fire: kindling (other poetry, books, memories, news articles, Wikipedia), oxygen (time to write, time to think without other media crowding out my thoughts), and a spark (the most mysterious part, but generally comes if I'm working at it aka writing, rather than waiting for it to happen). The more I write poetry, the quicker it is for the spark to catch. Which is not to say that it's easy, but it is faster than waiting for lightning."

Gloria Ogo, "Two Familiar Strangers"
"My process lives somewhere between routine and kairos. I try
to keep a steady rhythm of writing because showing up to the
page keeps the words moving, even on days when inspiration
feels far away. But then there are those rare kairotic moments,
when a line or image arrives so suddenly it feels like it's been
waiting for me all along, and I have to drop everything to chase
it. Routine keeps me grounded; kairos reminds me why I write in
the first place."

Rebecca Hart Olander, "The Last"
"I haven't always practiced writing on a regular schedule, but I
have been steadfast in my attention to poetry over time. I used
to think some muse had to hit me over the head to grace me
with an idea. Now I know it's necessary to, as Emily Dickinson
famously said in a letter, go 'out with lanterns looking for myself.'
For me this means cultivating fertile ground and creating sparks,
such as engaging in the poetry community, spending time in
artistic spaces or in nature, responding to prompts to get myself
generating, and reading the work of others."

Giulia Paglione, "At the post office"
"All my poetry happens for, within, about, and because of kairos.
I wait for those moments when something shifts. Sometimes I
chase them consciously, trying to capture an emotional truth as
it unfolds—but the best poems arrive unannounced. They can
strike anywhere: in a Byzantine church or while folding laundry
in my living room."

Danielle Salerno, "Meet Me at Burning Man"
"I try to create from routine, or at least, give myself the
opportunity to do so, though oftentimes I either don't like what
I've come up with, or I don't manage to come up with anything.
But I do think the more writing and creating is a habit, the easier
it is to have those moments of kairos to find inspiration."

Darah Schillinger, KAIROS guest editor
"I used to always wait for inspiration to strike to write but since graduating from my writing program I often find that kairos escapes me. Being inspired felt effortless when my main job was being a writing student and now it feels more like an errand after a long day of work than a need. When I fall into these moments of lackluster I usually look for inspiration in other pieces or poets I admire and see if a word or phrase stands out. I also have been forcing myself to write for the sake of writing by carving out intentional time, which is less productive than when I wait for inspiration, but keeps the muscles moving."

Hillary Smith-Maddern, "Intake Form After the 2024 Election"
"I have a writing routine. Or rather, I really attempt to maintain a writing routine in which I do some sort of daily writing-related task. My most visceral, sticky ideas tend to come naturally but I'm the kind of person who needs to have some sort of order in her life. I use my notes app to jot down any kairos that titillates my brain."

erica r. such, "In Defense of Career Suicide"
"Being a college student in a writing major, I am grateful for a structured routine to write where I am assigned a wide variety of modes and prompts to explore. However, when I am not in classes, I still see inspiration for my craft everywhere I go. I keep a running document on my phone of ideas for when I feel motivated to start a new project. Sometimes, I don't know I experienced a kairos moment until years after I experienced it. I'll have a kairos within a kairos moment of epiphany where I realize a long forgotten event was crucial to the person and writer I am today."

Vivian Walman-Randall, "Quilting"
"I do attempt to create my own routine, as I find that my inspiration is often there yet my urge to actually write is less. I tend to need the structure to get me to sit down and do it."

Kathleen Weed, "Blue Jacket"
"While I admire writers who create through sticking to a routine,
I find inspiration in being attentive to my wandering mind. I am
inclined to write when a phrase or puzzling perception persists in
my thoughts. I don't write because I have something to say. For
me, writing is an act of discovery."

Katharine Weinmann, "Right On Time"
"Crafting and editing poems for my forthcoming collection,
Skyborne Insight, Homemade Love, I developed a routine, writing
with a silent Zoom group early weekday mornings. When I blog,
I also typically set aside Sunday evening for a Monday drop and
later in the week for a Friday poem posting. Now it's been an
occasional response to inspiration's quiet nudge, knowing that
the extraverted, exuberant energy of the all-too-short Alberta
summers demands I take advantage. I've come to trust that once
home and settled from my annual autumn travels, I'm ready to
cocoon in my small studio and create. I've come to know that this
seasonal pattern is a surrender to the wisdom of kairos, coming
easier with age, where I need more quiet, more stillness, and
intentional slowing down to notice and to settle a nervous system
agitated by so much outer strife in the world."

Audrey J. Whitson, "In Sharp Relief"
"I set aside time for writing on a regular basis. At times this has
been daily (at one point I wrote on the bus to work), but often
it has been on weekends or on occasional retreats. I journal
sporadically, usually at the end of the day. I also have bursts of
insight, ideas, and words while 'averting my gaze' from the page,
especially when I walk in nature. I carry a notebook with me at
all times. My maxim: write everything down.

Keri Withington, "Southern Summer #5"
"My process includes some of both. I like routine in a lot of ways,
and I think that having a writing routine helps me to actually

make the time to write. I am busy with work, family, gardening, and other commitments beyond writing and so it is easy for writing to be the thing that is always put off for more urgent concerns. I have started adding writing to my to-do lists and trying to schedule time for a writing routine to make sure that I actually write, even if it's only for a few minutes. At the same time, my writing brain is always running in the background, like a crockpot that's just kind of cooking, even when I'm not paying attention to it. I don't always know when things will suddenly click. I also can't predict when something will spark a new idea. With the poem 'Southern Summer #5,' for example, I started writing it on the back of a receipt on my steering wheel while I was stuck in traffic by the lake. I jotted down a few lines and images for it, in a moment of inspiration, then I came back to those lines later to revise and build on them."

Chelsea Yates, "Jill"
"It's a mix of both. I find it essential to carve out regular writing time—even just a few minutes of freewriting each day—because if I wait to 'find time,' it never happens. I often turn to prompts to generate ideas (I especially like Lynda Barry's creative techniques and prompts, such as those outlined in her book *What It Is*— they're great for sparking memories to explore through writing.) Most of my freewrites don't go anywhere, but occasionally they lead to something worth developing. A few of my recent essays grew from that process. At the same time, inspiration sometimes arrives unexpectedly—through a song, a book, or, as with my essay 'Jill,' a conversation with a friend.

Kristin Camitta Zimet, "TIGERS"
"I trust myself to create, and I don't feel a need to make myself write on schedule. I am just always listening in case the ghost of a poem stirs, and I fling the door open to it. If a poem is coming in, everything else has to wait. So I am never without pen and paper. (This includes when I am driving, when I am sleeping,

and next to my beach shoes when I swim.) I know that tigers can yawn. Poems can leap out with the least provocation. When my little shoulder bag gets to feeling heavy, I empty it out. Last time, I found that I had squirreled away 20 pens."

Where do you find your time to create?

Contributors

Stephanie Anderson (she/they) is a library worker, union organizer, and mess of split ends in Baltimore, Maryland. They are the author of *SOMEONE ELSE'S FEELINGS* (Ghost City Press, 2025), with more of their work available in *BRUISER*, fifth wheel press, Artists from Maryland, *Libre*, *Burial Magazine*, and elsewhere. She's @whoastanderson everywhere, but she'd love you to sign her guestbook at whoastanderson.com.

Aileen Bassis is a visual artist and poet in New York City with a practice in book arts, printmaking, photography, and installation. She is the author of two chapbooks, *The Other Side of the Mirror* (Unlikely Books) and *Advice for Travelers and other poems* (Black Sunflowers Press). Her collection *Among Sinners and Saints* will be published in 2026 by Shanti Arts. She was awarded two poetry residencies to the Atlantic Center for the Arts, a fellowship in poetry to Yaddo Foundation, and grants in literature from the New York State Council on the Arts and the Queens Arts Fund.

Deepti Bhatia is a co-owner of a portrait photo studio in Chennai, India. She spends her free time reading ancient literature. Since the beginning of this year, she has penetrated the creative writing sphere. Her works so far have been published by *IHRAM* (Glasgow), *Kitaab*, *The Paris Post*, *The Wise Owl*, and *Delhi Poetry Slam*. She is also the Gold Medalist for the Monomousumi Creative Writing Contest February–March 2025.

Loretta Cantieri currently writes poetry, produces visual art, and is a volunteer with national and community organizations. She advocates for transgender rights and visibility. She hopes to somehow combine her engagement as a citizen with her creative self to lessen the teeter-totter sensation. She needs to be an octopus. Her poetry has been published in *Red Weather*, *Northern Narratives*, and most recently in a visual prose piece at Maypole Gallery in Chicago. She has an MFA from the California Institute of the Arts. She taught art at Minnesota State University Moorhead and Minnesota State Community and Technical College.

Roxanne Christiana is a retired psychologist and programmer living in Illinois. She returned to poetry in 2025 after many years away from writing and has been exploring how memory, science, and imagination intertwine. Her poems often move between the intimate and the cosmic, reflecting both personal experience and curiosity about the wider universe. Roxanne is an active member of the All Poetry community, where her work has been recognized with numerous contest placements and front-page features. "COLONIZING MARS" marks her first publication in a literary journal, and she is currently developing several chapbook projects.

Virginia Ottley Craighill lives in Sewanee, Tennessee, and Little Deer Isle, Maine. Her poems have appeared in *Colorado Review*, *NELLE*, and *Appalachian Review*. She has also had essays published in *The Sewanee Review* and *Best American Sports Writing* 2018.

Patricia Davis-Muffett (she/her) is author of the chapbook *Alchemy of Yeast and Tears*. Her work has won honors, including the 2024 Erskine J. Poetry Prize from Smartish Pace and Best of the Net and Pushcart Prize nominations, and appears in *Best American Poetry*, *Best New Poets*, and other publications. She lives in Rockville, Maryland.

Amy Devine is an artist from a lineage of artists whose work has been featured in several publications, including *The Antigonish Review*, *flashglass*, and Beyond the Veil Press. She is a Best of the Net nominee, and her first book, *Speaking of Bees*, was published by Harvard Square Press in 2025.

Johanna Elattar is a journalist and writer of Arab and European heritage, currently based in Hornell, New York. Her work explores the human stories behind history, culture, and conflict, blending investigative insight with literary sensitivity. Her writing has been featured in the *Hornell Sun*, *Wellsville Sun*, and Oxford University Press, which selected an excerpt of her work on missing and murdered Indigenous women for a forthcoming textbook. Johanna is deeply engaged with storytelling that examines resilience, identity, and the intersections of personal and collective history. She lives with her pets and continues to write both fiction and nonfiction.

Renee Emerson is the author of the poetry collections *Keeping Me Still* (Winter Goose Publishing, 2014), *Threshing Floor* (Jacar Press, 2016), and *Church Ladies* (Fernwood Press, 2023). She is also the author of the chapbook *The Commonplace Misfortunes of Everyday Plants* (Belle Point Press, 2023) and the middle grade novel *Why Silas Miller Must Learn to Ride a Bike* (Winter Goose Publishing, 2022). She lives in the Midwest with her husband and children. Find her on Substack at reneeemerson.substack.com.

Clara Garza is a 16-year-old writer and senior at California State University, Los Angeles. She serves as a politics and world health journalist with The Borgen Project and contributes editorially to numerous journals. Her creative and critical work has earned recognition across essay, photography, performance, and visual arts contests, including in statewide and national outlets like NOAA and KCACTF.

Pratibha Kumari Gupta is a writer with a keen eye for the intricate details of human experience and nature. Her work is a contemplative journey into themes of belonging, identity, and the archives of the heart. She is fascinated by the stories we tell and the ones we leave untold. She finds her muse in quiet observations and the complex root systems of relationships.

Taylor Harrison is an American writer. Her work has been featured or is forthcoming in a variety of literary magazines, including *P.O. BOX OUTER SPACE*, *Mulberry Literary*, *Cosmic Daffodil Journal*, *Yellow Arrow Journal*, and more. You can learn more about Taylor by following her on Instagram @tharrisonwriting.

Elizabeth Hazen is a poet and essayist. After teaching for 20 years, she changed tracks and now works at an independent bookstore. Her work has appeared in *Best American Poetry*, *Epoch*, *American Literary Review*, *Shenandoah*, and other journals. She has published two collections of poetry, *Chaos Theories* (2016) and *Girls Like Us* (2020). Her third collection, *The Sky Will Hold*, is forthcoming in March 2026. She lives in Baltimore, Maryland, with her family.

Jennifer Randall Hotz's work is featured or forthcoming in *Orange Blossom Review*, *Red Rock Review*, *Whale Road Review*, *Rust & Moth*, and *Naugatuck River Review*, among other publications. She won first place in poetry for the Virginia Writers Club 2023 Golden Nib Awards and was nominated for a 2024 Pushcart Prize. Find her at jenniferrandallhotz.com.

Cam McGlynn is a writer and scientific researcher living outside of Frederick, Maryland. Her work has appeared or is forthcoming in *Whale Road Review*, *Rattle* (online), *wildscape.*, *The Shore*, and *ONE ART*, among others. When not knee-deep in a swamp, you can find her on BlueSky @pinkpossumclub.bsky.social.

Gloria Ogo is an American-based Nigerian writer with several published novels and poetry collections. Her work has appeared in *Eye to the Telescope*, *Brittle Paper*, Spillwords Press, *MetaStellar*, *CỌN-SCÌÒ Magazine*, *Kaleidoscope*, *The Easterner*, *Daily Trust*, and more. With an MFA in creative writing, Gloria was a reader for *Barely South Review*. She is the winner of the Brigitte Poirson 2024 Literature Prize and finalist for the Jerri Dickseski Fiction Prize 2024 and ODU 2025 Poetry Prize, both with honorable mentions. Her work was also longlisted for the 2025 American Short(er) Fiction Prize. Find her online at glriaogo.wixsite.com/gloria-ogo.

Rebecca Hart Olander is a Women's National Book Association Poetry Award winner and the author of three poetry collections: *Dressing the Wounds* (dancing girl press, 2019), *Uncertain Acrobats* (CavanKerry Press, 2021), a finalist for the Eric Hoffer Book Award in poetry and the Massachusetts Book Award in poetry, and *Singing from the Deep End* (CavanKerry Press, 2026). Rebecca has taught writing at Amherst College, Smith College, and Westfield State University, and for the Pioneer Valley Writers' Workshop, and she works with poets in the Maslow Family Graduate Program in creative writing. She is the editor/director of Perugia Press.

Giulia Paglione is an Italian philologist and archaeologist from Rome, currently living between the United States and Greece. She holds a BA and MA in philology and is pursuing a PhD in Classics at the University of Cincinnati. Her poetry explores the liminal spaces between ancient and contemporary worlds, weaving together mythological reimaginings with intimate personal experience through a modern, feminist lens. Her recent creative work includes composing song-poems in Mycenaean Greek, reviving a Bronze Age language as a medium for contemporary poetic expression. Her work is forthcoming in the Italian magazine *Ellin Selae*.

Danielle Salerno (she/her) is a queer, ace writer and Jersey Girl currently sweltering in southwest Florida. Her work has been featured in *Azarão Lit Journal*, *The Cove Magazine*, Four Tulips Press, Arcana Poetry Press, *The Stars Diverged Journal*, *Poetic Reveries Magazine*, and *Cosmic Daffodil Journal* and is forthcoming in *Prudence Dispatch*, *Pearl Literary Magazine*, *Eunoia Review*, and *Moss Puppy Magazine*. When her nose is not firmly planted in her notebook, she can be found singing with the Fort Myers Symphonic Mastersingers and chasing her loved ones around with a Tarot deck. Find her on Instagram @xfild.poetry.

Darah Schillinger (she/her) is a writer based in Lexington Park, Maryland. Her poems have appeared in *AVATAR Literary Magazine*, *Yellow Arrow Journal*, *Maryland Bards Poetry Review*, *Empyrean Literary Magazine*, *Grub Street Magazine*, and *Eunoia Review* and on the Spillwords Press website. In October 2024 her poem "An elegy for the Pompeii woman the Internet wants to fuck" was named a finalist for the Montreal International Poetry Prize. Her first poetry chapbook, *when the daffodils die*, was released in July 2022 by Yellow Arrow Publishing. Her second collection, *Still Warm*, is a work in progress.

Hillary Smith-Maddern is an educator and committed dilettante. She enjoys diving into the shallow end of everything and scrolling casually through *JSTOR*. She aspires to fake her death and never return to America. She will obviously take her cats with her.

erica r. such is a Filipina poet, playwright, photographer, and sometimes actor based in Urbana, Illinois. She studies creative writing at the University of Illinois at Urbana-Champaign, where she will receive her BA in 2026.

Vivian Walman-Randall is a writer and scholar from southern California. She holds an MFA from Emerson College and a BA from the University of California, Santa Barbara, and is currently pursuing her PhD at Oklahoma State University. Her work can be read in *Spectrum Literary Journal, Summer Edition, The Catalyst*, and *Santa Barbara Literary Journal*. Vivian currently lives in Stillwater, Oklahoma, with her partner and their standard poodle, Clover.

Kathleen Weed is a licensed marriage and family therapist with advanced training in loss, grief, and meaning reconstruction. She lives in the San Francisco Bay Area. Kathleen's work has been published in *Yellow Arrow Journal, Bellevue Literary Review, The Grieving Garden, Living with the Death of a Child, The Dead Pets Poetry Anthology*, and *All Poems are Ghosts Poetry Anthology*. She writes for the joy of apprehending fleeting uncharted perceptions and attempting to shape them into meaningful art.

Katharine Weinmann, published internationally in literary journals and anthologies, writes poetry, walks long distances, and sees beauty in life's imperfections and photographs its shimmer. She was the 2024 winner of Canada's Lawrence House Centre for the Arts' Carmen Ziolkowski Poetry Prize and has been nominated for Best of the Net in poetry in 2026. Katharine blogs at awabisabilife.ca and lives on ᐊᒥᐢᑲᐧᒌᐧᐋᐢᑲᐦᐃᑲᐣ (Amiskwacîwâskahikan), Treaty 6 territory—the Canadian prairies—with her husband and their dog, Walker.

Audrey J. Whitson is the author of *Teaching Places, The Glorious Mysteries and Other Stories*, and most recently the author of a novel, *The Death of Annie the Water Witcher by Lightning*. She has an MA from the Graduate Theological Union at Berkeley University. Audrey was the 2023 writer in residence at MacEwan University and a mentor for the Writers' Guild of Alberta's Horizons Writing Circle in 2024. Writing is a spiritual practice for Audrey. Land is a constant presence in her work, as is a curiosity about other ways of being in the world. You can find her virtually at audreywhitson.com or out walking along the Kisiskâciwan-sîpî (North Saskatchewan River) in Treaty 6 territory, Edmonton, Alberta.

Keri Withington (she/her) is a poet, educator, and aspiring homesteader. Her poems have appeared in numerous journals and anthologies, recently including anthologies from White Stag Publishing. She has published two chapbooks, *Constellation of Freckles* (dancing girl press) and *Beckoning from the Waves* (Plan B Press). She lives with her husband, children, and a menagerie of pets in the Appalachian foothills. You can find her teaching for Pellissippi State, planting in her yard, hiking, or losing board games to her kids.

Chelsea Yates, originally from northeast Nebraska, lives in the Pacific Northwest and is a writer for the University of Washington. Her essays have appeared in *HerStry, The Good Life Review, Reunion: The Dallas Review*, and more. Find her at chelseayates.com.

Kristin Camitta Zimet is the author of *Take in My Arms the Dark*, a collection of poetry, and coauthor of *A Tender Time: Quaker Voices on the End of Life*. She was the long-time editor of *The Sow's Ear Poetry Review*. Her poems are in *Image, Sequestrum, Poet Lore*, and a great many other journals in 12 countries. They have been hung in art galleries and performed in concert halls.